Moments of Awareness

Moments of Awareness

INSPIRATIONAL VERSES

BY HELEN LOWRIE MARSHALL

WITH ILLUSTRATIONS

BY MURIEL WOOD

HALLMARK EDITIONS

Moments of Awareness

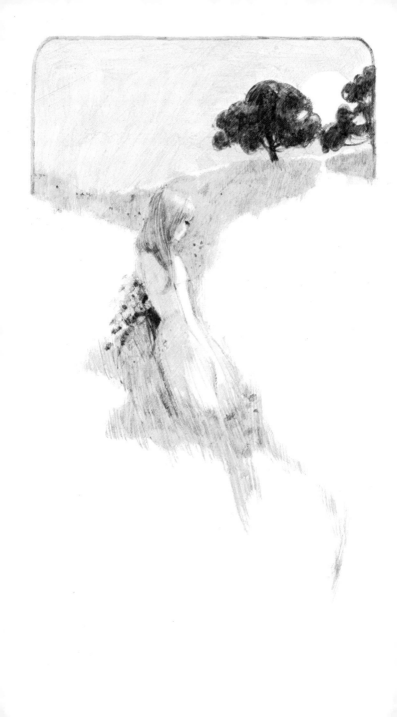

MOMENTS OF AWARENESS

So much of life we all pass by
With heedless ear, and careless eye.
Bent with our cares we plod along,
Blind to the beauty, deaf to the song.

But moments there are when we pause to rest
And turn our eyes from the goal's far crest.
We become aware of the wayside flowers,
And sense God's hand in this world of ours.

We hear a refrain, see a rainbow's end,
Or we look into the heart of a friend.
We feel at one with mankind. We share
His griefs and glories, joy and care.

The sun flecks gold through the sheltering trees,
And we shoulder our burdens with twice the ease.
Peace and content and a world that sings
The moment of true awareness brings.

GOOD MORNING

"Good Morning!" What a lovely way
  To open up a brand new day!
  Not knowing what that day may hold—
  A sun of tinsel or of gold—
  The phrase embraces in its scope
  The whole of man's eternal hope;
  His faith—of every soul a part;
  The love that lives in every heart.
"Good morning—and a Good Today!
  May all things happy come your way;
  And may the light of this new dawn
  Find all your cares and worries gone."
  So much the simple words convey—
"Good Morning—It's a lovely day!"

CLOSE TO THE HEART

Close to the heart is a secret place
Where dreams are stored away,
And sturdy candles of faith are kept
Against a darker day.

And there, too, are the memories—
The laughter shared, the tears,
The little things that mean so much,
Seen through the mist of years.

Our dearest wishes, deepest loves,
The burdens that we bear—
The essence of our being lies
In what we harbor there.

To each his own—a hideaway
That has no counterpart—
The treasure-house of the soul that lies
Somewhere close to the heart.

A SHAFT OF SUNLIGHT

A shaft of sunlight breaking through
Can make the whole world shining new;
Can shape tomorrow, change a life;
Can banish doubt and fear and strife.

One shaft of sunlight through the grey—
One word of cheer that we may say,
Could carry farflung consequence,
And might make all the difference.

NO FARTHER AWAY THAN TODAY

No farther away
Than Here and Today
Is the loveliest place I know—
A small secret spot
In a walled garden plot
Where all the nice memories grow.

It's bordered with kindness
And sprinkled with smiles
And shaded by friendly trees—
This small quiet place
In that walled garden space
With its bright little memories.

And I think about this—
How, if I were to miss
One day with my rake and my hoe
In planting the seeds
Of a few kindly deeds,
It would mean fewer memories to grow.

So I try every hour
To plant a new flower,
And strike down a weed in the way
Where the nice memories grow
In that spot that I know
No farther than Here and Today.

FOOTPRINTS IN THE SNOW

Spring tiptoed through the town last night,
Disguised in robes of winter-white.
This morning she seems far away—
The wind so cold—the skies so grey—
But there are signs that prove it so,
Small crocus footprints in the snow!

LITTLE THINGS

Dear God, please give to me
A thankful heart for little things—
For sunshine on my kitchen floor,
For news the postman brings;
For memories in the making,
Things the children do and say,
That I will smile about, perhaps,
Some future, lonelier day.

Grant me appreciation
Of the small joys that are mine—
The children's birthday parties,
My honeysuckle vine;
The clean, fresh smell
Of clothes just washed;
The ivy on my wall,
The children's thrilled delight
To wake and find the first snowfall.
For robins in the springtime,
And autumn's crispy weather—
For leaves that crunch,
Friends in for lunch
And laughter shared together.

Give me enthusiasm
To greet each brand new day
With an honest joy in living
As I go my simple way;
I do not ask contentment
That would ambition stay—
But let me love the little things
I find along the way.

A LOVELY DAY

Actually, I couldn't say
What made this such a lovely day.
The air was chill, the clouds hung low,
Yet it was lovely—that I know.
Perhaps it was because someone
Smiled my way and brought the sun;
Maybe it was only that
A friend stopped for a little chat;
Or that a neighbor passing by
Called a warm and friendly "Hi!"
Possibly its special glow
Came from helping one I know—
Not much really—Just a hand
To let him know I understand.
Nothing happened, actually,
To set this day apart for me.
Things went along the usual way—
But oh, it's been a lovely day!

SACRAMENTS OF DAILY LIVING

Each day, upon my daily round,
I find myself on holy ground—
The morning-glories on my fence
Inspire quiet reverence.
Just one small, tender seedling grew,
And now, this miracle in blue.
A robin in the apple tree
Sings out his glad doxology.
I hear the pure, unsullied joy
Of laughter from a little boy;
I bow before the firm belief
And faith of one who lives with grief;
I watch a jet plane skim the skies
And marvel at man's enterprise;
I look upon a field of wheat
And thank God for the bread we eat;
I watch the benedictive rain
On low-bowed heads of flower and grain.
A friend drops in, a neighbor calls,
The lamps are lit, night gently falls;
Contentment settles with the sun
In labors of the day well done.
So many little altars there,
So many simple calls to prayer,
So many reasons for thanksgiving—
The sacraments of daily living.

LOOK UP AND LIVE

This business of living was meant to be more
    Than plodding along each day
With head bowed down and eyes on the ground
    While Time ticks the hours away.

God made this world a delightful place
    With beauty everywhere—
The grass, the flowers, the trees, the sky,
    The tang of clean, fresh air—

A world to be lived in, laughed in, loved,
    To be met with joy and zest,
A world with a challenge for each of us
    To give it our very best.

This business of living was never meant
    As a treadmill sort of thing;
There are rivers to cross, and mountains to climb,
    And glorious songs to sing!

MY CAMEOS OF MEMORY

These are my treasures kept apart,
Cradled in velvet in my heart,
Graven profiles, picture-clear,
Perfect moments, priceless-dear,
Etched in ageless time to be
   My cameos of memory.

The hours I have spent with you,
The tender times, the fun times, too,
The summer roses and the rain,
The laughter and the precious pain
Of loving you—your loving me—
   My cameos of memory.

These are my wealth, my warmth, my light,
I keep them dream-close all the night.
With finger-tips of heart and mind
I trace each profile there defined—
These treasures none can take from me—
   My cameos of memory.

ISN'T LIFE GLORIOUS

Isn't life glorious! Isn't it grand!
Here—take it—hold it tight in your hand;
Squeeze every drop of it into your soul,
Drink of the joy of it, sun-sweet and whole!
Laugh with the love of it, burst into song!
Scatter its richness as you stride along!
Isn't life splendid—and isn't it great
We can always start living—it's never too late!

The Pattern of Life

LIKE A PATCHWORK QUILT

Life isn't given us all of a piece;
    It's more like a patchwork quilt—
Each hour and minute a patch to fit in
    To the pattern that's being built.

With some patches gay—and some patches dark,
    And some that seem ever so dull—
But if we were given to set some apart,
    We'd hardly know which to cull.

For it takes the dark patches to set off the light,
    And the dull to show up the gay—
And, somehow, the pattern just wouldn't be right
    If we took any part away.

No, life isn't given us all of a piece,
    But in patches of hours to use,
That each can work out his pattern of life
    To whatever design he might choose.

ONE DAY AT A TIME

I'm glad life is given us bit by bit,
    In minutes, and days, and years;
For if we were faced with the whole of it
    How filled it would be with fears;
With all of its laughter, and all of its pain,
    Its sorrow and joy and care—
Why, even its beauty all at one time
    Would be more than we could bear.

But God drops a bit of happiness here,
    And lowers a shadow there,
And each of us has his portion of both,
    The bitter and the fair.
And, whether the way be rough or fine,
    It's a comforting thing to know
We've only one step to take at a time,
    Just one little day to go.

ALWAYS THE SPRING

Life has its seasons—its bright summer days,
Its autumns made poignant with memories' haze,
Its cold, lonely winters when bitter winds blow—
But always the crocus of Hope in the snow.

Always the day when the morning breaks through
And clouds break away to a skyful of blue.
Life has its seasons—its sun and its rain,
Its winter—but always the springtime again!

THOUGHTS IN A GARDEN

Today, as I worked in my garden,
  I thought what a fine thing 'twould be
If each of us could pluck the weeds
  From our garden of memory.
If all of the harsh and ugly thoughts
  And every unkind deed
Could be tossed aside, and the barren spots
  Replaced with fresh new seed.

And I thought, if we could visualize
  The memories to grow
Out of the seeds we're planting—
  We'd live differently, I know;
We'd have more time for things worthwhile,
  The finer things, I'm sure,
And we'd plant the seed of a friendly smile
  Where a frown-weed grew before.

We'd give less thought to life's humdrum cares
  That seem to have no end,
And we'd learn the interest an hour bears
  When invested in a friend.
And oh, I know, if we could see—
  As true as stars above—
What tomorrow's memories would be,
  We'd have more time for love!

ONLY INCHES AWAY

Life is measured by inches,
By steps taken one at a time,
Not by the height of the peak we seek,
But each little rise we climb.

The span of our life is measured
Minute by minute—not years;
We live in a very small world of our own
In a vast universe of spheres.

Yes, life is measured by inches,
But inches can add up to far;
A light-year is only inches away—
We can inch our way up to a star!

THE SONG AND THE ECHO

A song we sing. We cannot know
How far the sound of it will go,
How long its echo will be heard.
We can but pray that every word,
Each note in this, the song we sing,
Will find its resting place and bring
Some little measure of repose,
Some strength, some happiness to those
Who hear our song. If just one smiles
To hear its echo down the miles,
Then we should be content and know
Our song was meant—God willed it so.

LIVING STILL

A garden is a growing thing.
    Each day, each passing hour,
Some bit of newness there unfolds—
    A leaf, a bud, a flower.
A garden is a living thing,
    And even when the snow
Has blanketed its silent form
    It does not cease to grow,
For every tender seedling there,
    Each hard, encrusted pod,
Contains a tiny spark of life,
    A living bit of God.

Life, also, is a growing thing;
    Each day, each passing hour,
Finds something new unfolding there—
    New thoughts, new strength, new power.
And when the snows of sorrow come,
    As snows of sorrow will,
The seeds of Hope lie dormant then
    But go on living still.
And, just as Spring returns to bring
    The garden fresh new leaves—
So does the Spring of Life return
    To every heart that grieves.

THE SONG OF LIFE

The music of life is played by ear,
Each heart improvising its own,
Setting the tempo and choosing the key
In major or minor tone.

No printed score is provided,
And no two tunes the same;
And if our song is discordant,
We've only ourselves to blame.

For the keyboard of life holds beauty—
There's harmony waiting there
For the heart that attunes its song of life
To peace, goodwill and prayer.

AFTERGLOW

I'd like the memory of me
To be a happy one.
I'd like to leave an afterglow
Of smiles when day is done.

I'd like to leave an echo
Whispering softly down the ways,
Of happy times, and laughing times
And bright and sunny days.

I'd like the tears of those who grieve
To dry before the sun
Of happy memories I leave
Behind—when day is done.

A Faith to Live By

A FAITH TO LIVE BY

Give me the faith of adventure, Lord,
 The courage to try the new,
The will to press on in spite of the dark,
 Knowing I walk with You.

Give me the faith of desire and hope,
 The inward urge to achieve,
All things are possible with You.
 O Lord, let me believe!

Give me the faith of awareness
 Of beauty everywhere,
Eyes to see, and ears to hear—
 An open heart to care.

Give me a faith to live by,
 Joyous and unafraid.
A glorious faith to match the dawn
 Of this day You have made!

HEAVEN-TALL

I'm such a little person, Lord,
    So very small,
Yet when I reach my soul to Thee,
    I'm Heaven-tall.

My tasks are all so trivial,
    Such drudgery,
Yet each is touched with nobleness
    When done for Thee.

A life time seems so empty-short,
    The hours flee—
Yet in Thy hands life reaches to
    Eternity.

BY ANY OTHER NAME

To seek the heights and depths of thought
  And pause in silence there;
Some call it meditation—
  I like to call it prayer.

To look out on the troubled world
  And find the true and fair;
Some call it contemplation—
  I like to call it prayer.

To give oneself for others,
  To lift and love and share,
Some call it consecration—
  I like to call it prayer.

To sense a silent, reverent awe
  At beauty everywhere;
Some call it adoration—
  I like to call it prayer.

GOD'S SYMPHONY

God plays His symphony
Upon the heartstrings—yours and mine;
With gentle, knowing touch
He weaves His harmony divine;
And if, sometimes, harsh discord
Makes that harmony unfair,
If war and strife and bitterness
Confuse the peaceful air,
'Tis not God's lack of artistry
Nor symphony grown dim,
But, rather, that our hearts have fallen
Out of tune with Him.

THINK ON THESE THINGS

If you are ever plagued with doubt,
And question whether God's about,
Try thinking on some simple things;
You'll be surprised the peace it brings—
A sleeping child; a summer's day;
A puppy, awkward in its play;
The clean, washed air that follows rain;
A diamond-frosted window pane;
An apple tree all pink and white;
The stillness of a starlit night;
A fire crackling on the hearth;
The smell of freshly spaded earth;
A trail you knew once long ago;
A picket fence high-capped with snow;
A song your mother used to sing—
Why you can pick most anything
And you will find your answer there—
It's still God's world—He's everywhere!

THE GREATEST OF THESE

Reason faces up to life,
And sees things as they are;

Hope sees things as they ought to be,
And wishes on a star;

Faith dreams of miracles to come
That only God can do;

Love goes to work with patient hands
To make these dreams come true.

WHATEVER YOUR GIFT

What is that you hold in your hand?
Nothing, you say? Look again.
Every hand holds some special gift—
A hammer, a broom, a pen,
A hoe, a scalpel, an artist's brush,
A needle, a microscope,
A violin's bow, a way with words
In the giving of faith and hope.
What is that you hold in your hand?
Whatever your gift may be,
It can open your door to abundant life—
You hold in your hand the key.

ALONG THE WAY

We cannot all be ministers
And preach with learned phrase;
Nor can we all be soloists
With golden song of praise;
But we can live a sermon here
And we can live a song,
And neither song nor sermon
Need be either loud or long;
But quietly, in little things
We do from day to day—
Some simple, kindly deed,
Some word of comfort we may say—
And, even though we're unaware
That such has been our goal,
Somewhere along the way an angel
Writes, "He saved a soul!"

BEYOND MEASURE

How can one measure friendship—
The firm, warm clasp of a hand,
The comfort in the welcome sound
Of the words, "I understand"?

How can one measure courage—
The strength we find to fight,
To suffer life's anxieties,
To stand up for the right?

How can one measure beauty, hope,
Or happiness, or love?
What man-made measure can encompass
Faith in God above?

So much of life—the best of life—
The things we truly treasure,
And these, the gifts of boundless depth
Beyond all earthly measure.

BETTER SHARED

Some things are better shared—
    A grief, a joy,
A meal, an open fire,
    A book, a toy—
Yes, some things must be shared
    To fully please—
And our own faith is not
    The least of these.

MORNING PRAYER

Good morning, Lord,
    Another lovely day—
Help me to keep it so,
    Dear Lord, I pray.

May no small, careless word
    Or deed of mine
Let fall a shadow there
    To spoil the shine;

No act of kindness,
    Thoughtlessly undone,
Make dim this lovely morning's
    Bright, clean sun.

Help me to keep this day
    As good as new,
Till at its close I give
    It back to you.

SHARE IT

If grief is yours,
Turn to a friend and share it;
An understanding heart
Will help you bear it.
And if joy fills your heart
Let others share
Your happiness, as well
As your despair.

If faith is yours,
A peace profound and deep,
Let it not be a secret
That you keep
Enshrined, but shrouded,
In your inmost heart—
Tell others, let the whole world
Have a part.

GRATEFUL

I'm grateful for the privilege of prayer,
Grateful I can call and know He's there;
Grateful for the peace that floods my soul,
For the strength to press on toward the goal,
For the faith that banishes all doubt,
For the hope that puts my fears to rout;
Grateful for the sweet surcease from care—
Grateful for the privilege of prayer.

KEEP A DREAM IN THE MAKING

Keep some little dream in the making
If youth you would like to hold.
Old Father Time is defeated by dreams—
A dreamer never grows old.

For dreams have a way of quickening
The heart, and the years pass you by.
You can always tell the man with a dream
By the ageless gleam in his eye.

So keep a small dream in the making.
It needn't be big or bold—
Just some little dream to beckon you on
And you'll never, no never, grow old.

ARE YOU FISHING FOR DREAMS?

Are you fishing for dreams? Then bait your hook
    With a bit of reality,
Then swing out wide and cast your line
    Far out into Life's sea.

Let every dream have a fighting chance,
    Give it plenty of slack,
But settle for only the biggest and best—
    Throw the little ones back.

Are you fishing for dreams? Then I wish you luck,
    It's a good dream-fishing day,
May you catch a beauty—but oh, take care,
    Lest the big one get away.

AIM FOR A STAR

Aim for a star! Never be satisfied
With a life that is less than the best,
Failure lies only in not having tried—
In keeping the soul suppressed.

Aim for a star! Look up and away,
And follow its beckoning beam.
Make each Tomorrow a better Today—
And don't be afraid to dream.

Aim for a star, and keep your sights high!
With a heartful of faith within,
Your feet on the ground, and your eyes on the sky,
Some day you are bound to win!

THE REAL YOU

Don't be afraid to see yourself
    As the you-that-you'd-like-to-be,
No matter how far removed from the real
    The you-of-your-dreams may be.

Keep dreaming the dream—hitch a ride on a star,
    Hold tight—never let yourself fall,
And one day you'll find that the you-of-your-dreams
    Is the you-that-is-real, after all.

BRIGHT HORIZONS

We should be glad for distant things,
For beauty 'round the bend;
For highways that lead on and on
With never any end.
Be glad for goals just out of reach,
The challenge of a star,
The glory of a distant light
That beckons from afar.
For hopes and dreams are built on
That enchanted distant mile,
And far off bright horizons
Make the road today worthwhile.

NO REGRETS

Never regret a ride on a star,
A dream, or a hope that was aimed too far;
That wonderful castle you built in the air,
Though it tumbled and left but a memory there.
For dreams that go drifting,
And hopes that are high—
A ride on a star through a silvery sky—
These are the wonderful, magical things,
These are the glorious, gossamer wings
That carry us up where the angels play,
And Heaven is ours—though it's only a day;
But one day in Heaven has infinite worth
In brightening the practical pathways of earth.

HOLD TO YOUR DREAM

A dream is a high and lovely thing,
A heart-flown kite on the winds of Spring.
Buoyant and bright, it hovers there
Against the blue—Almost a prayer,
Calling the spirit to broaden its scope
Of faith in the future, and courage, and hope;
Adding dimensions of height and girth
To even the simplest joys of earth.

If you have a dream, oh, how lucky you are!
Play out the string and let it sail far,
But follow it—ever so close—with your eyes,
For dreams have been known to be lost in the skies.
Never lose sight of it—hold fast the string—
A dream is a precious and wonderful thing!

REACH HIGH!

Reach high! The finest things of life
Are on the topmost shelves.
We have to stand on tiptoe—
Stretch our small, self-centered selves;
We have to look above our heads
To where the heart can see,
If we would reach that finer life
We'd like our life to be.

We have to mount our old mistakes
And try and try again
If we would even touch
Life's highest moments now and then—
If we would even brush with lightest
Fingertips the best
That life on earth can offer—
If we would reach the crest.

Reach high! The best is always kept
Upon life's topmost shelves,
But not beyond our reach if we
Will reach beyond our selves.

DARE TO BE HAPPY

Dare to be happy—don't shy away,
Reach out and capture the joy of Today!

Life is for living! Give it a try;
Open your heart to that sun in the sky.

Dare to be loving, and trusting, and true;
Treasure the hours with those dear to you.

Dare to be kind—it's more fun than you know;
Give joy to others, and watch your own grow.

Dare to admit all your blessings, and then
Every day count them all over again.

Dare to be happy, don't be afraid—
This is the day which the Lord hath made!

EVERYBODY DREAMS

Everybody dreams—
The very young, the very old;
Everybody has a secret
Dream he's never told,
Everybody, at some time,
Has wished upon a star,
Blown out the candles on a cake,
Had hopes that drifted far.
Everybody dreams—
And dreams so often don't come true,
But I think life is better
For the dreams we have,
                              Don't you?

Set at The Castle Press in Linotype Aldus, a roman with
old-face characteristics, designed by Hermann Zapf.
Aldus was named for the 16th century Venetian
printer Aldus Manutius.
Printed on Hallmark Eggshell Book paper.
Designed by Harald Peter.